£4·95

INTRODUCTION

GW00367553

The ability to sight-read fluently is a most important part of your instrumental training. Yet the *study* of sight-reading is often badly neglected by young players and is frequently regarded as no more than a rather unpleasant side-line. If you become a *good* sight-reader you will be able to learn pieces more quickly, and play in ensembles with confidence and assurance. Also, in grade examinations, good performance in the sight-reading test will result in useful extra marks!

Using the workbook

The purpose of this workbook is to incorporate sight-reading regularly into your practice and lessons, and to help you prepare for the sight-reading test in grade examinations. It offers you a progressive series of enjoyable and stimulating stages in which, with careful work, you should show considerable improvement from week to week.

Each stage consists of two parts: firstly, exercises which you should prepare in advance, along with a short piece with questions; and secondly, an unprepared test, to be found at the end of the book.

Your teacher will mark your work according to accuracy. Each stage carries a maximum of 50 marks and your work will be assessed as follows:

> 2 marks for each of the six questions relating to the prepared piece (total 12).
> 18 marks for the prepared piece itself.
> 20 marks for the unprepared test. (Teachers should devise a similar series of questions for the unprepared test, and take the answers into account when allocating a final mark.)

Space is given at the end of each stage for you to keep a running total of your marks as you progress. If you are scoring 40 or more each time you are doing well!

At the top of the first page in each stage you will see one or two new features to be introduced. There are then normally four different types of exercise:

1 **Rhythmic exercises** It is very important that you should be able to feel and maintain a steady beat. These exercises will help develop this ability. There are at least four ways of doing them: clap or tap the lower line (the beat) while singing the upper line to 'la'; tap the lower line with your foot and clap the upper line; on a table or flat surface, tap the lower line with one hand and the upper line with the other; 'play' the lower line on a metronome and clap or tap the upper line.

2 **Melodic exercises** Fluent sight-reading depends on recognising melodic shapes at first glance. These shapes are often related to scales and arpeggios. Before you begin, always notice the *key-signature* and the notes affected by it, along with any accidentals.

3 **A prepared piece with questions** You should prepare carefully both the piece and the questions, which are to help you think about and understand the piece before you play it. Put your answers in the spaces provided.

4 **An unprepared piece** Finally, your teacher will give you an *unprepared* test to be read at *sight*. Make sure you have read the *Sight-reading Checklist* on page 22 before you begin each piece.

Remember to count throughout each piece and to keep going at a steady and even tempo. Always try to look ahead, at least to the next note or beat.

4

STAGE 1

RHYTHMIC EXERCISES
Always note and remember the time- and key-signatures.

MELODIC EXERCISES

This book is copyright. Photocopying is illegal.

PREPARED PIECE

1 How many beats are there in each bar? ☐

2 What is the key of this piece? ☐

3 How many beats is each crotchet (♩) worth? ☐

4 How many beats is each crotchet rest (𝄽) worth? ☐

5 What does *Moderato* mean? ☐

6 What does **f** *(forte)* indicate? ☐

* Total: ☐

Moderato

Mark: ☐

Prepared work total: ☐

Unprepared: ☐

Total: ☐

* The mark boxes throughout are to be filled in by the teacher.

STAGE 2

Accidentals

RHYTHMIC EXERCISES

1

2

3

MELODIC EXERCISES

1

2

3

4

5

PREPARED PIECE

1 How many beats are there in each bar?

2 What are the letter names of the notes in bars 6 and 7?

3 How many beats is each crochet (♩) worth?

4 How many beats is each minim (𝅗𝅥) worth?

5 What does *Moderato* mean?

6 What does ***f*** *(forte)* indicate?

Total:

Moderato

Mark:

Prepared work total:

Unprepared:

Total:

Running totals:

1	2

STAGE 3

$\frac{3}{4}$ 𝅗𝅥.

RHYTHMIC EXERCISES

MELODIC EXERCISES

PREPARED PIECE

1 What does $\frac{3}{4}$ indicate? ☐

2 How many beats is each minim (𝅗𝅥) worth? ☐

3 How many beats is each dotted minim (𝅗𝅥.) worth? ☐

4 What is the letter name of the first note in bar 13? ☐

5 What does *mf* *(mezzo-forte)* indicate? ☐

6 What is the meaning of *Andante*? ☐

Total: ☐

Andante

Mark: ☐

Prepared work total: ☐

Unprepared: ☐

Total: ☐

Running totals:

1	2	3

STAGE 4

RHYTHMIC EXERCISES

MELODIC EXERCISES

PREPARED PIECE

1 How many beats is each dotted minim (𝅗𝅥.) worth? □

2 Mark any notes affected by the key-signature. □

3 How many beats does this rest ▬ occupy? □

4 What does *p* *(piano)* indicate? □

5 What does ◁ ▷ indicate? □

6 What is the meaning of *Andantino?* □

Total: □

Andantino

Mark: □

Prepared work total: □

Unprepared: □

Total: □

Running totals:

1	2	3	4

STAGE 5

RHYTHMIC EXERCISES

MELODIC EXERCISES

PREPARED PIECE

1 What does **4/4** indicate?

2 Clap the following rhythm:

3 What do *mf* and *p* indicate?

4 In which key is the piece written?

5 What does the sign ◁ *(crescendo)* indicate?

6 What is the meaning of *Allegro moderato?*

Total:

Allegro moderato

Mark:

Prepared work total:

Unprepared:

Total:

Running totals:

1	2	3	4	5

STAGE 6

A minor ♩

RHYTHMIC EXERCISES

MELODIC EXERCISES

PREPARED PIECE

1 In which key is the piece written?

2 Mark any accidentals with a cross.

3 How many beats are there in each bar?

4 What is the letter name of the first note in bar 4?

bar 5?

bar 7?

5 What is the meaning of *Moderato con moto*?

6 What do *dim. (diminuendo)* and *cresc. (crescendo)* indicate?

Total:

Moderato con moto

Mark:

Prepared work total:

Unprepared:

Total:

Running totals:

1	2	3	4	5	6

STAGE 7

RHYTHMIC EXERCISES

MELODIC EXERCISES

PREPARED PIECE

1 How many beats are there in each bar?

2 In which key is the piece written?

3 Mark with a cross the notes affected by the key-signature.

4 What does the mark > in bar 3 mean?

5 Clap this rhythm

6 Mark an accidental with an asterisk.

Total:

Andante grazioso

Mark:

Prepared work total:

Unprepared:

Total:

Running totals:

1	2	3	4	5	6	7

STAGE 8

RHYTHMIC EXERCISES

MELODIC EXERCISES

PREPARED PIECE

1 In which key is the piece written? ☐

2 Mark the C sharps with a cross. ☐

3 What do the dots under and over the notes indicate? ☐

4 What does *Allegretto* mean? ☐

5 What does *cresc. (crescendo)* indicate? ☐

6 Mark a tied note with an asterisk. ☐

Total: ☐

Mark: ☐

Prepared work total: ☐

Unprepared: ☐

Total: ☐

Running totals:

1	2	3	4	5	6	7	8

STAGE 9

RHYTHMIC EXERCISES

1

2

3

MELODIC EXERCISES

1

2

3

4

PREPARED PIECE

1 What are the clues that will help you identify the character of this piece?

2 How will you achieve a musical performance?

3 In which key is this piece written?

4 Mark with a bracket two bars in which notes of the arpeggio of D minor occur.

5 What does *Andantino* mean?

6 Clap this rhythm

Total:

Andantino

Mark:

Prepared work total:

Unprepared:

Total:

Running totals:

1	2	3	4	5	6	7	8	9

A SIGHT-READING CHECKLIST

Before you begin to play a piece at sight, always remember to consider the following:

1   Look at the key-signature, and find the notes which need raising or lowering.

2   Look at the time-signature, and decide how you will count the piece.

3   Notice any accidentals that may occur.

4   Notice the scale and arpeggio patterns.

5   Work out ledger-line notes if necessary.

6   Notice dynamic and other markings.

7   Look at the tempo mark and decide what speed to play.

8   Count one bar before you begin, to establish the speed.

When performing your sight-reading piece, always remember to:

1   CONTINUE TO COUNT THROUGHOUT THE PIECE.

2   Keep going at a steady and even tempo.

3   Ignore mistakes.

4   Check the key-signature at the beginning of each new line.

5   Look ahead - at least to the next beat or note.

6   Play *musically*.

UNPREPARED TESTS
STAGE 1

STAGE 2

1 Moderato

2 Andante

3 Lento

STAGE 3

STAGE 4

STAGE 5

STAGE 6

STAGE 7

STAGE 8